Fact Finders®

CAUSE AND EFFECT

TO Preserve THE UNION

CAUSES AND EFFECTS

of the Missouri Compromise

BY KAAVONIA HINTON

Consultant:
William E. Foley
Professor Emeritus of History
University of Central Missouri
Warrensburg, Missouri

CAPSTONE PRESS
a capstone imprint

Fact Finders Books are published by Capstone Press,
1710 Roe Crest Drive, North Mankato, Minnesota 56003
www.capstonepub.com

Library of Congress Cataloging-in-Publication Data
Hinton, KaaVonia
To preserve the Union : causes and effects of the Missouri compromise/by
KaaVonia Hinton.
pages cm—(Fact finders—cause and effect)
Includes bibliographical references and index.
Summary: "Explains the Missouri Compromise and its impact"—Provided by
publisher.
ISBN 978-1-4765-0238-0 (library binding)—ISBN 978-1-4765-3404-6 (pbk.)—
ISBN 978-1-4765-3412-1 (ebook pdf)
1. Missouri compromise—Juvenile literature. 2. Slavery—United States—History—
Juvenile literature. 3. United States—Politics and government—1815–1861—Juvenile
literature. I. Title.
E373.H56 2014
973.5'4—dc23   2013008340

Editorial Credits
Jennifer Besel, editor; Alison Thiele, designer; Svetlana Zhurkin, media researcher;
    Laura Manthe, production specialist

Photo Credits
Bridgeman Art Library: Corcoran Gallery of Art, Washington, D.C., U.S.A., 13; Library
of Congress, cover (inset), 5, 10–11, 14, 17, 18, 27, 29; National Archives and Records
Administration: Our Documents, 16; Newscom: Picture History, 8, 15; North Wind
Picture Archives, cover (middle), 21, 24; Shutterstock: Onur Ersin, 19; Wikimedia, 12;
Wikipedia: U.S. Army, 22

Printed in the United States of America in Brainerd, Minnesota.
032013   007721BANGF13

Table OF CONTENTS

A Growing PROBLEM

In the 1800s the issue of slavery was tearing the United States apart. Some people believed they had a right to own slaves. Others felt slavery should be illegal. This great divide only worsened as the country grew.

In 1803 President Thomas Jefferson purchased the Louisiana Territory. People began to move west in great numbers. Soon those people wanted the territories to become states. Some wanted slavery to be legal in the new states. Others did not want slavery to spread west. Heated fighting broke out among the people and in **Congress**. Lawmakers tried to settle the problem with the Missouri Compromise. This agreement would change the country forever.

Congress: the government body of the United States that makes laws, made up of the Senate and the House of Representatives

People in Southern states relied on slave labor to run their large farms. Many Northern states had made slavery illegal. The disagreement over slavery deeply divided the United States.

What Caused the MISSOURI COMPROMISE?

By the late 1700s, the slave trade was big business in the American **colonies**. Slaves were captured in Africa and the West Indies. Then they were sold to slave owners in America. Many people disagreed with using slave labor, even at this time. But the Revolutionary War (1775–1783) overshadowed the debate. Colonists fought for their freedom from Great Britain. When they won, they had to develop a new country with a government and laws. And they had to address slavery.

Cause #1—Northwest Ordinance

Congress passed the Northwest Ordinance in July 1787. This law provided a plan for areas in the Northwest Territory to become states.

The law also made slavery illegal in the Northwest Territory. **Citizens** living north of the Ohio River could not own slaves. But people south of the Ohio could.

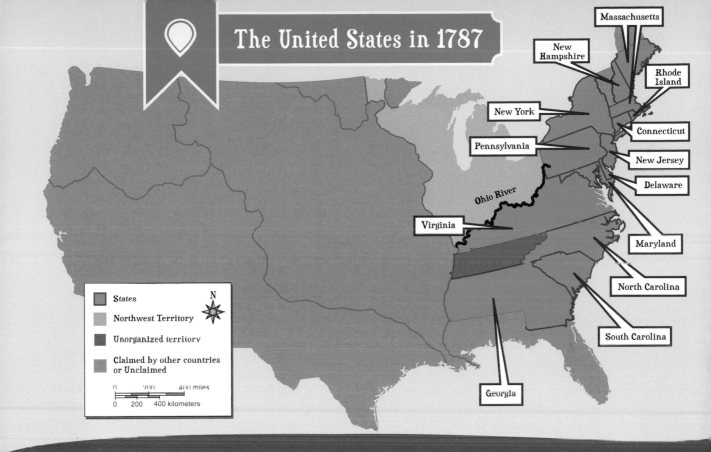

The United States in 1787

Massachusetts

New Hampshire

Rhode Island

New York

Connecticut

Pennsylvania

New Jersey

Delaware

Ohio River

Virginia

Maryland

North Carolina

South Carolina

Georgia

States

Northwest Territory

Unorganized territory

Claimed by other countries or Unclaimed

N

| 0 | 200 | 400 miles |

| 0 | 200 | 400 kilometers |

At the time, this division seemed like a good idea. Northern leaders who opposed slavery had limited its spread. Southern leaders were pleased too. They believed that without slaves, midwestern farmers could not grow enough tobacco to compete with southern plantations. But dividing the country between slave and free states would have deep and lasting consequences.

colony: a place that is settled by people from another country and is controlled by that country

citizen: a member of a country or state who has the right to live there

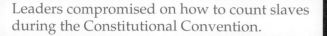

Leaders compromised on how to count slaves during the Constitutional Convention.

Cause #2—Slavery in the Constitution

Just two months after signing the Northwest Ordinance, leaders signed the U.S. Constitution. Once again slavery became a sticking point.

While developing the Constitution, leaders decided a state's **population** would determine two things. First it affected how many lawmakers each state had in the House of Representatives. Population also determined how much a state would pay in taxes.

population: the number of people living in a certain place

But slaves were an issue. Southern states might pay less in taxes if slaves weren't counted. After much discussion, Southerners agreed to count a slave as three-fifths of a person. This compromise still allowed Southern states to pay less in taxes. However it also gave them fewer representatives and less power to create laws they wanted.

Neither side was totally happy with the decision. It did little to ease the growing tension between Northern and Southern states. In fact, it made it worse.

FAST FACT: By 1860 about 4 million slaves lived in the Southern slave states.

Counting People: Whites vs. Slaves

3 people   1 4/5 people

1 white person counted as 1 person.
1 slave counted as 3/5 of a person.

Cause #3—Westward Expansion

In 1803 President Thomas Jefferson purchased the Louisiana Territory from France. People soon began moving west. The Northwest Ordinance had made slavery illegal north of the Ohio River. So as new states joined the **Union**, it was fairly easy to determine if the state would allow slavery.

But then came Missouri. Jefferson wanted to allow slavery in the Missouri Territory. By 1818 slave owners had brought at least 10,000 slaves to the area. But when Missouri applied for statehood, Congress was at odds. Some parts of the Missouri Territory were north of the Ohio River. But other parts of it lay to the south.

FAST FACT: The Louisiana Purchase doubled the size of the United States.

Union: the United States of America

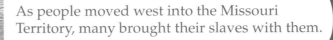

As people moved west into the Missouri Territory, many brought their slaves with them.

Cause #4—Tipping the Balance

While lawmakers were figuring out the Missouri issue, Alabama applied to be a state. They easily admitted Alabama as a slave state because it was far south of the Ohio River. This addition meant there was an equal number of free and slave states. Missouri's statehood would destroy that balance.

Northerners panicked. If slave states outnumbered free states, they would have more power in Congress. Many Northern lawmakers wanted to stop that from happening.

Trying to Agree

Lawmakers fiercely argued over the issue of Missouri. Tempers boiled over when Representative James Tallmadge of New York introduced his idea. Tallmadge wanted to add an **amendment** to the Missouri bill. His amendment would grant Missouri statehood if no more slaves were brought into the area. Missouri would also have to free all the children of slaves born after Missouri became a state.

Southerners hated the idea. They said Tallmadge's amendment was a plan to end slavery. Outraged Southerners warned they would leave the Union to protect slavery.

Representative James Tallmadge

amendment: a change made to a law or a legal document

Lawmakers gave passionate speeches to Congress supporting and opposing the Tallmadge Amendment.

Voting on the Tallmadge Amendment

The House of Representatives passed the Tallmadge amendment, 79 to 67. But the amendment did not pass in the Senate. Senators there were not willing to break the equal balance of free and slave states. Missouri's statehood was at a standstill. But the division and anger between the North and South continued to grow.

Known as the great compromiser, Henry Clay worked tirelessly to find a solution to the Missouri issue.

The Maine Event

During the next session of Congress, Maine applied for statehood. Maine was far north of the Ohio River and could easily be admitted as a free state. Speaker of the House Henry Clay argued that Maine and Missouri should be admitted together. With this plan the balance between slave and free states would stay the same. Clay hoped this compromise would help the nation avoid a **civil war**.

Clay's plan seemed like a solution. But Northern and Southern leaders had to be convinced. After weeks of debating and arguing, the Senators came to an agreement. Maine and Missouri would be admitted to the Union together. But they added two additional rules to the bill. First, slavery would not be allowed in parts of the Louisiana Territory that were north of Missouri's southern border. Second, any escaped slaves found in the area could be reclaimed and sent back to their owners.

One of the additional rules in the Missouri Compromise made it law that runaway slaves should be returned to their owners if found.

SLAVE HANDCUFFS AND LEG IRONS

$150 REWARD.

RANAWAY from the subscriber, on the night of Monday the 11th July, a negro man named

TOM,

about 30 years of age, 5 feet 6 or 7 inches high; of dark color; heavy in the chest; several of his jaw teeth out; and upon his body are several old marks of the whip, one of them straight down the back. He took with him a quantity of clothing, and several hats.

A reward of $150 will be paid for his apprehension and security, if taken out of the State of Kentucky; $100 if taken in any county bordering on the Ohio river; $50 if taken in any of the interior counties except Fayette; or $20 if taken in the latter county.
july 12-84-tf

B. L. BOSTON.

civil war: war between opposing groups within one country

Clay tried to get the House of Representatives to agree to the Missouri bill. He spoke for hours about Missouri's rights. He said that the United States would eventually end slavery. Nothing helped.

Frustrated, Clay formed a committee to handle the problem. The committee suggested that the bill be broken into three. One bill would admit Missouri as a slave state. Another bill would add Maine as a free state. A third bill would address slavery in the rest of the Louisiana Territory. Splitting the bill allowed lawmakers to vote for the parts they wanted to support. Finally the House voted and passed the bills. The Missouri Compromise was law.

the Missouri Compromise of 1820

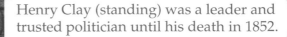
Henry Clay (standing) was a leader and trusted politician until his death in 1852.

The Great Compromiser

Henry Clay is known as the great compromiser because of his leadership during the Missouri Compromise. Clay was a successful lawyer in Kentucky. He inherited and bought slaves of his own. But despite owning slaves, he always argued that slavery was wrong. He even tried to convince people in Kentucky that slavery should end slowly. Concerns about slavery troubled Clay all of his life. When he died in 1852, his will freed the children of the slaves he owned. He also directed they be sent to live in Africa.

Not So Fast

Everyone thought the Missouri issue was finally settled. All Missouri had to do was write a constitution. Then Congress could make it an official state.

But after all the fighting in Congress, Missouri's leaders were frustrated. Missourians believed Congress had overstepped its rights. They thought the state should choose if it would be a free or slave state. So in its constitution, Missouri declared that free African-Americans could not live there.

Alexander McNair was governor of Missouri from 1820 to 1824. He also signed Missouri's constitution in 1820.

States are not allowed to make rules that go against laws set up in the U.S. Constitution.

Fighting in Congress started up again. Some said Missouri's constitution went against the national one. The U.S. Constitution said citizens could settle in any state. Since free African-Americans were citizens of some states, they said Missouri must allow them to live there.

Is It a State or Not?

Despite the disagreement over its constitution, the Senate admitted Missouri as a state. But the House did not. Lawmakers continued fighting. Southerners threatened to leave the Union. To them slavery was important to their way of life. They valued it more than keeping the country together. It seemed like the nation was falling apart.

Missouri's citizens were more frustrated than ever. They believed they should be a state, and they decided to act like one. A presidential election was held in 1820. Missouri cast votes in the **electoral college**. Northerners were outraged. They said Missouri was not a state, so it had no votes. Lawmakers actually had shouting matches over their disagreement.

They settled their fight over the election by counting the votes twice. They counted Missouri's votes in one count. They left Missouri out in another count. But it didn't really matter. President James Monroe was the only candidate.

electoral college: a group of people who elect the U.S. president; each state is given a certain number of electoral votes; the candidate who receives the most votes from the people is awarded the state's electoral votes

Shouting matches and fist fights happened often in Congress in the 1800s.

⟩

FAST FACT: Missouri was technically not a state at the time of the 1820 election. Both the House and Senate have to approve a state's constitution before it's admitted as a state.

William Eustis

The Second Missouri Compromise

By 1821 the Missouri fight had been going on for almost three years. Lawmakers were frustrated and angry. Some Southern leaders began to grow suspicious of Northern leaders. They claimed that Northern lawmakers had gotten Maine as a free state. So now they weren't going to keep their word and admit Missouri.

On January 24, 1821, William Eustis of Massachusetts suggested another compromise. He said Missouri should simply remove the part in its constitution that **banned** free African-Americans from the state. Henry Clay moved that the lawmaker's idea be accepted. But most of the lawmakers voted against Eustis' idea.

Clay was worried. He warned again that denying Missouri statehood could cause Southern states to leave the Union. The following month, Clay suggested that another committee find a solution. Clay argued that Missouri should be admitted if its constitution allowed all citizens to settle there. Clay also encouraged committee members to ask other lawmakers to approve Missouri's constitution.

Clay and the committee members spoke with lawmakers in private. One by one, they convinced leaders to admit Missouri if it promised not to take away the rights of citizens. Their work paid off. Lawmakers voted, and both the House and Senate voted yes. Missouri would be a state.

ban: to forbid or make something illegal

What Effects Did THE MISSOURI COMPROMISE HAVE?

The Missouri Compromise, and the fighting that went into getting it passed, deeply affected the United States.

Effect #1—Limited the Spread of Slavery

The Missouri Compromise did not solve the problem of slavery. But it did limit its spread. The bill set a new line for where slavery would be allowed. Any new state created north of Missouri's southern border would be free.

The Missouri Compromise limited slavery to Southern states.

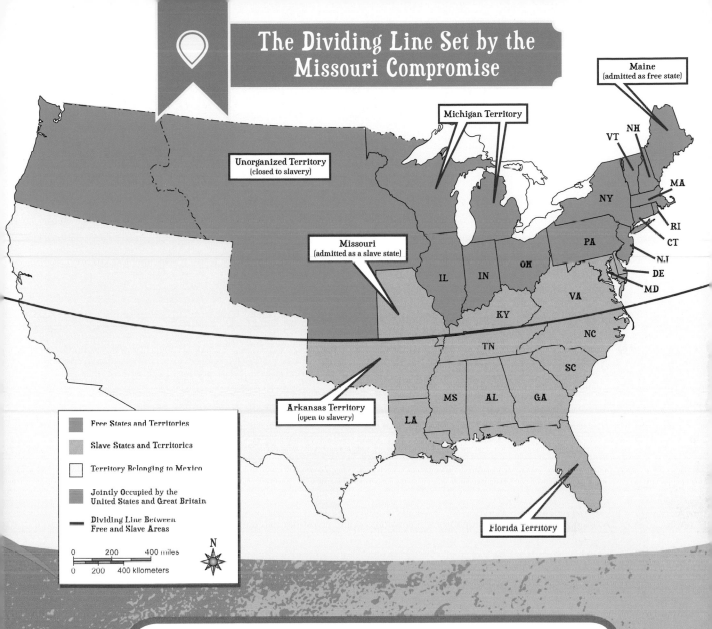

The Dividing Line Set by the Missouri Compromise

Maine
(admitted as free state)

Michigan Territory

NH
VT
MA
NY
RI
CT
NJ
DE
MD

Unorganized Territory
(closed to slavery)

PA

OH

Missouri
(admitted as a slave state)

IL   IN

VA

KY

NC

TN

SC

Arkansas Territory
(open to slavery)

MS   AL   GA

LA

Florida Territory

Free States and Territories

Slave States and Territories

Territory Belonging to Mexico

Jointly Occupied by the United States and Great Britain

Dividing Line Between Free and Slave Areas

0   200   400 miles

0   200   400 kilometers

N

Without this rule, slavery may have spread into northern territories. With the Missouri Compromise in place, the country was clearly divided between Northern free states and Southern slave states.

Effect #2—Increased Tension

Though Northerners and Southerners accepted the compromise, they said it was flawed. Northerners thought slavery should be banned from Missouri. Southerners believed the compromise insulted their way of life. Instead of unifying the country, the fight over slavery continued.

The Kansas-Nebraska Act

In 1854 Senator Stephen Douglas introduced the Kansas-Nebraska Act. This act would make two new territories out of land west of the Missouri River. Douglas needed the support of Southern leaders to pass the bill. So he included a rule that said settlers would decide if the state had slavery. This rule went directly against the Missouri Compromise. Douglas' bill created an uproar in Congress. But President Franklin Pierce supported the bill, and eventually it became law. This act destroyed the Missouri Compromise.

The Dred Scott Decision

Dred Scott was a slave. He lived with his owner, John Emerson, in Missouri, where slavery was legal. But later Emerson and Scott moved to Illinois and Wisconsin, where slavery was illegal.

After Emerson died, Scott sued Emerson's wife for his freedom. Scott claimed that since he had lived in Illinois and Wisconsin, he should be a free man. The case went to the U.S. Supreme Court.

Dred Scott

In 1857 the court said African-Americans, whether they were slave or free, could not be U.S. citizens. It denied Scott his freedom. The court also said the Missouri Compromise was **unconstitutional**. The decision killed the Missouri Compromise for good.

unconstitutional: a law that goes against something in the Constitution

Effect #3—Delayed War but Couldn't Stop It

During the debates over Missouri's statehood, many Southern states threatened to leave the Union. The compromise kept the Union together ... at least for a time.

The Kansas-Nebraska Act and Dred Scott ruling **repealed** the compromise after nearly 30 years. Tension was at a boiling point. Then in 1860 Abraham Lincoln was elected president. Southern states were convinced he would try to end slavery. They left the Union, and the country went to war.

The Missouri Compromise did not directly cause the U.S. Civil War. It delayed Southern states from leaving the Union in the 1820s. But it also caused a great divide in the country—a division that led to war.

Cause and Effect

The Missouri Compromise was a major turning point in American history. Leaders were forced to discuss the issue of slavery. Their compromise did not solve the issue. But it did make people aware that a permanent decision would have to be made.

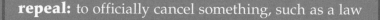
repeal: to officially cancel something, such as a law

The Civil War was fought over slavery and states' rights. The Missouri Compromise could not prevent the war, but it did delay it.

GLOSSARY

amendment (uh-MEND-muhnt)—a change made to a law or a legal document

ban (BAN)—to forbid or make something illegal

citizen (SI-tuh-zuhn)—a member of a country or state who has the right to live there

civil war (SIV-il WOR)—a war between different sections or parties of the same country or nation

colony (KAH-luh-nee)—a place that is settled by people from another country and is controlled by that country

Congress (KAHNG-gruhs)—the government body of the United States that makes laws, made up of the Senate and the House of Representatives

electoral college (ee-lehk-TOHR-uhl KAH-luhj)—a group of people who elect the U.S. president; each state is given a certain number of electoral votes; the candidate who receives the most votes from the people is awarded the state's electoral votes

population (pop-yuh-LAY-shuhn)—the number of people living in a certain place

repeal (ri-PEEL)—to officially cancel something, such as a law

unconstitutional (uhn-kon-stuh-TOO-shuh-nuhl)—a law that goes against something in the Constitution

Union (YOON-yuhn)—the United States of America; also the Northern states that fought against the Southern states in the Civil War

READ MORE

Collins, Terry. *Into the West: Causes and Effects of Westward Expansion.* Cause and Effect. North Mankato, Minn.: Capstone Press, 2014.

De Medeiros, James. *Slavery.* Black History. New York: AV2 by Weigl, 2013.

Lanier, Wendy. *What Was the Missouri Compromise? And Other Questions about the Struggle over Slavery.* Six Questions of American History. Minneapolis: Lerner Publications, 2012.

INTERNET SITES

FactHound offers a safe, fun way to find Internet sites related to this book. All of the sites on FactHound have been researched by our staff.

Here's all you do:

Visit *www.facthound.com*

Type in this code: 9781476502380

Check out projects, games and lots more at
www.capstonekids.com

CRITICAL THINKING USING THE COMMON CORE

1. Think about what happened in Congress during the Missouri Compromise. How was that similar to what happens in Congress today? How was it different? If you need to, examine other texts to support your findings. (Integration of Knowledge and Ideas)

2. Did the Missouri Compromise have any lasting effects? Support your answer. (Key Ideas and Details)

INDEX